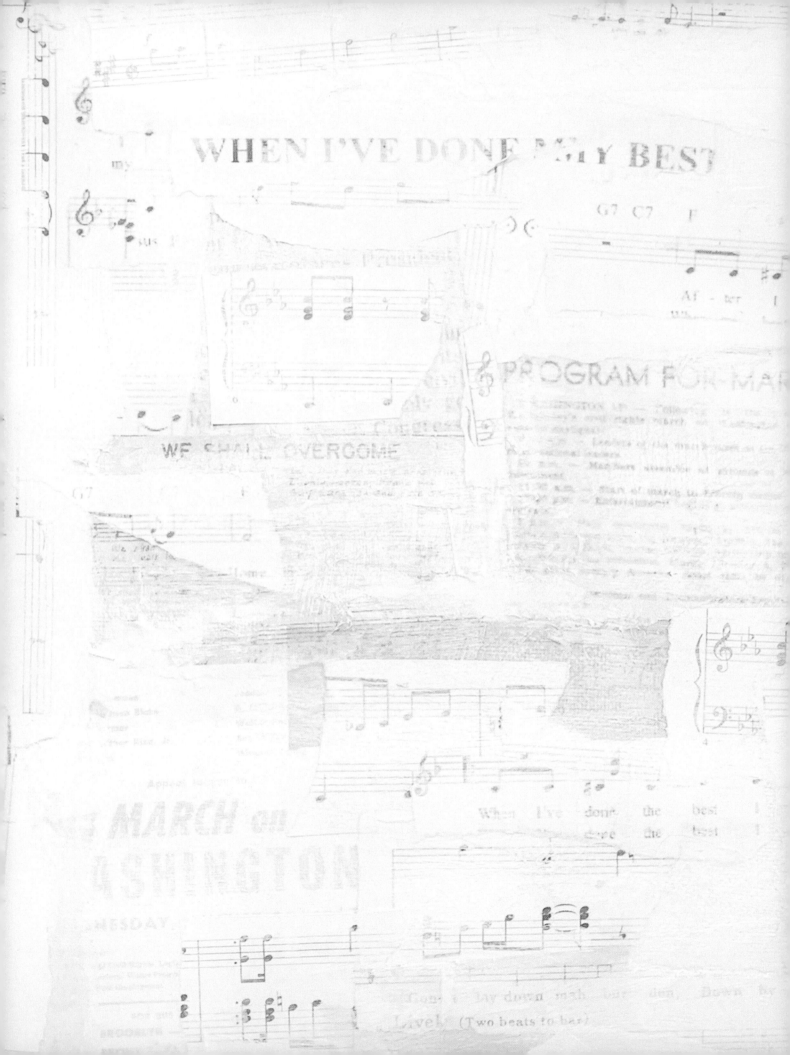

A SONG FOR THE UNSUNG

Bayard Rustin, the Man Behind the 1963 March on Washington

By **Carole Boston Weatherford** & **Rob Sanders**

Illustrated by **Byron McCray**

Henry Holt and Company
New York

*W*hat Bayard Rustin saw on the morning of August 28, 1963, was not what he expected.

Quiet stillness echoed off the Washington Monument.

The steady beat of Bayard's footsteps mingled with the voices of security guards, reporters, and a handful of others.

Where were the crowds of protesters he had worked so hard to bring to Washington, D.C.? For eight weeks he'd been orchestrating the protest, hoping to bring a hundred thousand to the nation's capital.

The moment had almost arrived for the March on Washington for Jobs and Freedom. Where were the protesters? Bayard had faith that the crowds would arrive.

Sing "My Lord, What a Morning" as the sun rises over the nation's capital.

Sing "Pray On" to call on the hopes of the ancestors.

Born in West Chester, Pennsylvania, in 1912,
Bayard had the faith of his grandmother Julia Davis
Rustin. She taught young Bayard her Quaker values.

Early on, he learned the church's teachings,
including a belief in nonviolence.

Bayard was also learning about the injustices
that African Americans faced.

Julia supported the National Association for
the Advancement of Colored People (NAACP).

Young Bayard gave up his bed when well-known
NAACP members stayed overnight in the Rustin home.

He heard the grown-ups talking late into the night
about the civil rights struggle.

Sing "Nobody Knows the Trouble I've Seen"
under the burden of racism.

Sing "Lift Every Voice and Sing," the Negro national anthem, to draw on the strength of those freedom fighters.

By the time he went to college, Bayard had developed firm beliefs and a mighty singing voice.

On tour with a quartet, he performed spirituals, work songs, and the blues. His vibrant tenor tones brought listeners to tears.

A reporter spotted Bayard. He asked the question Bayard must have been thinking—"Where are the crowds?"

Bayard pulled a piece of paper from his pocket, examined it, then replied, "Everything is right on schedule."

What the reporter didn't know was that the paper was blank. Perhaps Bayard's hopes were as empty as that sheet of paper.

Sing "Ain't Gonna Let Nobody Turn Me 'Round" to the doubters.

As a young man, Bayard's feelings about justice, peace, and nonviolence grew stronger and stronger.

And he put his feelings about equality and pacifism into action.

Sing "Every Time I Feel the Spirit" to keep the faith.

When he refused to give up his seat on a bus, Bayard was beaten and arrested. He did not fight back.

Sing "Traveling Shoes" to take a stand by sitting down.

When he refused to fight in World War II or to support the war, Bayard was sent to prison for more than two years.

Behind bars, he spoke up for equality, working to integrate the prison so Black and white prisoners were treated equally.

Sing "Down by the Riverside" to advocate for peace.

Sing "The Gospel Train" along the first-ever freedom ride.

Once out of prison, Bayard joined another protest against segregated buses. Again, he was arrested. This time he was sentenced to a chain gang.

But the harsh treatment did not change Bayard's commitment to civil rights and his dedication to peaceful protest.

Sing "I'm Gonna Sit at the Welcome Table" to demand service.

When Bayard staged a one-man sit-in at a whites-only lunch counter, he was again arrested. But jail time didn't stop him from fighting for what he knew was right.

As a young Black gay man, Bayard Rustin was also learning about another kind of inequality and injustice.

Back then, men who loved men and women who loved women could not socialize together. Doing so could get you arrested. Bayard knew that firsthand. And revealing that you were gay could mean losing your job, your friends, or even your family.

Bayard's family stood by him, but being gay threatened his civil rights mission.

Some African American leaders didn't want to work with him.

Some white lawmakers tried to shame him.

Still, Bayard kept on fighting for equality. And he did so while being nonviolent.

Sing "I've Been 'Buked" when society frowns on who you are.

Sing "When I've Done the Best I Can"
when the hour has come.

Under the leadership of A. Philip Randolph and with the help of a small staff, Bayard worked long hours to make sure every last detail of the march was planned.

Letters were written. Calls made. Money raised.

Posters, banners, and buttons were created.

Buses, carpools, trains, and planes were scheduled.

Maps were drawn.

Volunteers were in place.

Speakers and singers were enlisted.

All the preparations for the March on Washington were complete. Security guards. Portable restrooms. First-aid stations. Drinking water. Even 80,000 box lunches had been prepared.

Of course, the best preparations in the world could not guarantee that the march would be peaceful.

Bayard knew that peaceful protest was often met with violence.

Years earlier, Bayard had traveled to India to learn about nonviolent protest from the followers of Mahatma Gandhi.

Bayard put what he learned into practice. He protested injustice around the world and back home in the United States.

After Rosa Parks was arrested for not giving up her bus seat to a white man, Bayard went to Montgomery, Alabama. There, he introduced Dr. Martin Luther King, Jr., to the power of peaceful protest.

When Dr. King led the Montgomery bus boycott, nonviolence was at the center. From then on, the Civil Rights Movement would preach and practice peaceful protest.

Sing "I've Got Peace Like a River" to commit to nonviolent resistance.

Sing *"When the Saints Go Marching In"*
as thousands from across the nation arrive
at the National Mall.

WE
DEMAND
DECENT
HOUSING
NOW!

WE
DEMAND
AN END
TO
POLICE
BRUTALITY
NOW!

WE
MARCH
FOR
JOBS FOR ALL
A DECENT
PAY!

We Demand
THE RIGHT
TO VOTE
EVERY-
WHERE

By 9:00 a.m. on August 28, 1963, 40,000 people gathered at the Washington Monument.

By 10:30, the number had grown to 90,000.

Bayard's work was paying off.

And people kept coming.

They came by car and train, on planes and buses, and even on foot.

More people kept arriving—until 250,000 stood beneath the blazing summer sun.

Led by Dr. King, the march began around noon.

With him walked men and women, young and old, Black and white, rich and poor.

They walked side by side. Hand in hand. Row by row.

Some walked silently. Others buzzed with excitement.

Some carried their children. Some carried signs.

End Segregation Rules

Voting Rights Now!

Let Us Rise Together and Be One Free People

One row behind Dr. King marched Bayard Rustin.

A gay Black man.

The man responsible for orchestrating the march.

Sing "Walk Together, Children" as protesters march along the mile-long route.

Bayard was used to not being in the spotlight.

His name had been left off important reports he had coauthored.

He had been a trusted adviser to Dr. King and then had been let go.

Some would have nothing to do with Bayard. *After all*, they must have thought, *what does a gay man have to offer us or our cause?*

But when A. Philip Randolph was put in charge of the March on Washington, he knew immediately the man he wanted as his deputy.

Bayard Rustin.

Sing "This Little Light of Mine" from behind the scenes.

Bayard did not have time to think about any of that as the crowd of
marchers arrived at the Lincoln Memorial and spilled out into the Mall.
Bare feet dangled in the reflecting pool.
People munched on box lunches.

Sing "If I Had a Hammer" to tear down walls that divide us.

Sing "We Shall Overcome," hand in hand, as folk singer

Sing "When the Spirit
Says Sing."

Bayard had carefully composed the program for the
March on Washington. Each song. Each speaker.
The speakers inspired. The singers performed.
The crowd listened and cheered, clapped and chanted.

Music had always been at the center of Bayard's life.
Songs from church.
Songs sung with a college quartet.
Songs he wrote, sang, and recorded.
Prison songs and chain-gang songs.
The songs of the countries he visited.
The songs of the people he met.
Songs of peace. Songs of protest.

The day built to a crescendo as the final speaker—
Dr. Martin Luther King, Jr.—came before the crowd.

Bayard knew Dr. King was the perfect speaker to end the
program.

But the speech that Dr. King gave was even more
powerful than Bayard had hoped it would be.

The speech hit a high note with the rousing refrain—
"I have a dream . . ."

During the speech, Bayard stood in the background
as he had done so many times before.

He listened. He nodded.

In front of him stood a mosaic of Americans, most of
whom did not know his name. Or his role in bringing
them together on that historic day.

Sing "He's Got the Whole World in His Hands" as opera star Marian Anderson blesses the crowd with her rich contralto.

After the applause for Dr. King died down, Bayard stepped from the background and up to the podium.

He faced the crowd and spoke into the microphone.

"Friends," he said, "at five o'clock today the leaders whom you have heard will go to President Kennedy to carry the demands of this revolution. It is now time for you to act."

One by one, Bayard read the demands of the march.

Again and again, the crowd cheered, "YES!"

The 250,000 marchers left that day committed to work, vote, and protest nonviolently for civil rights.

Thousands of reporters, photographers, and other members of the media shared the story of the peaceful march with America and the world.

The monumental march led to the passing of the Civil Rights Act of 1964. That law ended segregation in public places and banned employment discrimination.

A quiet man orchestrated it all.

A man behind a movement.

An unsung hero.

A gay African American.

Bayard Rustin.

Finally, a song for you.

Sing "Ain't That Good News" when day is finally done.

BAYARD RUSTIN—1912-1987

Bayard was raised by his grandparents Julia and Janifer Rustin. Janifer was an African Methodist Episcopalian and Julia was a Quaker. Bayard was raised in both traditions, but his core values came from the Quaker influences. He was a pacifist, a labor organizer, an African American, and a gay man. Bayard traveled to India to study nonviolent protest with those who worked with Mahatma Gandhi. He later introduced those tactics to Dr. Martin Luther King, Jr. Nonviolence became central to the Civil Rights Movement and other protest movements as well.

Bayard was often discriminated against for being gay, but that did not stop him from being one of the key organizers of the March on Washington for Jobs and Freedom on August 28, 1963. Throughout his life, Bayard continued to advocate for civil rights, workers' rights, human rights, and gay rights. He died in New York City on August 24, 1987, at the age of 75. In 2013, Bayard was posthumously awarded with the Presidential Medal of Freedom by President Barack Obama.

BAYARD RUSTIN TIMELINE*

1912	Born in West Chester, Pennsylvania
1932	Graduated from West Chester High School
1932	Attended Wilberforce University
1934	Attended Cheyney State Teachers College
1937	Joined the American Friends Service Committee Peace Brigade
1937	Moved to Harlem, New York City
1941	Joined the Fellowship of Reconciliation
1942	Beaten and arrested for sitting in whites-only section of bus
1944	Sent to prison for refusing to participate in World War II
1946	Released from prison
1947	Participated in the Journey of Reconciliation
1948	Traveled to India and learned more about nonviolent protest from Gandhi's followers
1949	Served on a chain gang in North Carolina for his participation in bus integration
1956	Assisted Dr. King with the Montgomery bus boycott
1960	Removed from Dr. King's circle of advisers
1963	Organized the March on Washington for Jobs and Freedom
1964	Civil Rights Act passed
1964	Became the executive director of the A. Philip Randolph Institute
1986	Testified for gay rights bill in New York City
1987	Died in New York City
2013	Awarded the Presidential Medal of Freedom by President Barack Obama

*Adapted from *Bayard Rustin: The Invisible Activist* by Jacqueline Houtman, Walter Naegle, and Michael G. Long (Philadelphia, PA: Quaker Press of FCG, 2014).

MARCH ON WASHINGTON FOR JOBS AND FREEDOM
AUGUST 28, 1963

LINCOLN MEMORIAL PROGRAM

1. The National Anthem — Led by Marian Anderson.
2. Invocation — The Very Rev. Patrick O'Boyle, *Archbishop of Washington.*
3. Opening Remarks — A. Philip Randolph, *Director March on Washington for Jobs and Freedom.*
4. Remarks — Dr. Eugene Carson Blake, *Stated Clerk, United Presbyterian Church of the U.S.A.; Vice Chairman, Commission on Race Relations of the National Council of Churches of Christ in America.*
5. Tribute to Negro Women Fighters for Freedom — Mrs. Medgar Evers
    Daisy Bates
    Diane Nash Bevel
    Mrs. Medgar Evers
    Mrs. Herbert Lee
    Rosa Parks
    Gloria Richardson
6. Remarks — John Lewis, *National Chairman, Student Nonviolent Coordinating Committee.*
7. Remarks — Walter Reuther, *President, United Automobile, Aerospace and Agricultural Implement Wokers of America, AFL-CIO; Chairman, Industrial Union Department, AFL-CIO.*
8. Remarks — James Farmer, *National Director, Congress of Racial Equality.*
9. Selection — Eva Jessye Choir
10. Prayer — Rabbi Uri Miller, *President Synagogue Council of America.*
11. Remarks — Whitney M. Young, Jr., *Executive Director, National Urban League.*
12. Remarks — Mathew Ahmann, *Executive Director, National Catholic Conference for Interracial Justice.*
13. Remarks — Roy Wilkins, *Executive Secretary, National Association for the Advancement of Colored People.*
14. Selection — Miss Mahalia Jackson
15. Remarks — Rabbi Joachim Prinz, *President American Jewish Congress.*
16. Remarks — The Rev. Dr. Martin Luther King, Jr., *President, Southern Christian Leadership Conference.*
17. The Pledge — A. Philip Randolph
18. Benediction — Dr. Benjamin E. Mays, *President, Morehouse College.*

"WE SHALL OVERCOME"

THE OFFICIAL PROGRAM FOR THE MARCH ON WASHINGTON FOR JOBS AND FREEDOM

Source: Our Documents, https://www.ourdocuments.gov/doc.php?flash=false&doc=96

Watch and listen to Bayard's speech at the March on Washington:

https://www.youtube.com/watch?v=KW7urLULT9k

http://openvault.wgbh.org/catalog/A_27BB06E300874F279030125D1216C8B5#at_61.615_s

THE HISTORY OF PEACEFUL PROTEST*

The 1950s and 1960s witnessed a new form of protest in America—nonviolent, peaceful protest. The movement was rooted in the philosophies of Henry David Thoreau, who in 1849 wrote the essay "Civil Disobedience." Mohandas K. Gandhi—who was given the title *Mahatma* (great-souled) in 1914—practiced the principles of nonviolence in India in the 1930s. Dr. Martin Luther King, Jr., is credited for advocating for the use of peaceful protest during the civil rights era of the 1960s. Dr. King had been introduced to peaceful protest by Bayard Rustin.

In 1957, King gave a speech titled "The Power of Nonviolence." Even before that time, he had begun teaching about the philosophy and using it in protests for African American civil rights. American labor leader Cesar Chavez used nonviolent protests in the 1960s to organize farm-workers and, later, to gain rights for Hispanics. Those Civil Rights Movements were followed not only by peaceful antiwar protests, but also by protests for women's rights, gay rights, the environment, voter rights, and more.

Not all peaceful protests are organized by large groups. When a person votes, he or she might actually be protesting. Sometimes people write a letter to express an opinion, sing a song of protest, or stop buying certain products or shopping at certain stores, while others might buy a product to show their support for a particular view. Some wear a T-shirt or a button, place a bumper sticker on their car, knit a hat, post on social media, or fly a flag to share their views and opinions in nonviolent ways. Others might light a candle, meditate about positive changes they wish to see, or pray. Some people file lawsuits in the hopes of overturning laws or creating new ones.

According to Dr. King, the ultimate goal of nonviolent protest is "not [to] humiliate or defeat the opponent but to win his friendship and understanding." He said that the outcome of nonviolent protest would be "reconciliation and the creation of a beloved community."

*Adapted from *Peaceful Fights for Equal Rights* by Rob Sanders (New York: Simon & Schuster Books for Young Readers, 2018).

THE MUSIC BEHIND THE MOVEMENT

Music played a vital role in the Civil Rights Movement. During marches and rallies, protesters sang to unify with one another and to uplift themselves. They also sang freedom songs as they faced harassment, brutality, arrest, and imprisonment. While "We Shall Overcome" was the unofficial anthem of the movement, protesters also created new songs and changed the lyrics of spirituals, gospel songs, and rhythm-and-blues tunes to fit the moment. These protest songs conveyed a message of hope and justice to the world.

We Shall Overcome

(Public Domain)

We shall overcome

We shall overcome

We shall overcome, some day

Oh, deep in my heart

I do believe

We shall overcome, some day

THE 10 DEMANDS OF THE MARCH ON WASHINGTON FOR JOBS AND FREEDOM

1. Comprehensive and effective *civil rights legislation* from the present Congress—without compromise or filibuster—to guarantee all Americans
    access to all public accommodations
    decent housing
    adequate and integrated education
    the right to vote

2. Withholding of Federal funds from all programs in which discrimination exists.

3. *Desegregation of all school districts in 1963.*

4. Enforcement of the *Fourteenth Amendment*—reducing Congressional representation of states where citizens are disfranchised.

5. A new *Executive Order* banning discrimination in all housing supported by federal funds.

6. Authority for the Attorney General to institute *injunctive suits* when any Constitutional right is violated.

7. A massive federal program to train and place all unemployed workers—Negro and white—on meaningful and dignified jobs at decent wages.

8. A national *minimum* wage act that will give all Americans a decent standard of living. (Government surveys show that anything less than $2.00 an hour fails to do this.)

9. A broadened *Fair Labor Standards Act* to include all areas of employment which are presently excluded.

10. A federal *Fair Employment Practices Act* barring discrimination by federal, state, and municipal governments, and by employers, contractors, employment agencies, and trade unions.

Source: March on Washington, Organizing Manual No. 2, https://www.crmvet.org/docs/moworg2.pdf

READ MORE ABOUT DR. MARTIN LUTHER KING, JR., THE MARCH ON WASHINGTON FOR JOBS AND FREEDOM, AND PEACEFUL PROTEST

A Picture Book of Martin Luther King, Jr., by David A. Adler and Robert Casilla. New York: Holiday House, 1989.

A Sweet Smell of Roses by Angela Johnson and Eric Velazquez. New York: Simon & Schuster Books for Young Readers, 2007.

Be a King: Dr. Martin Luther King Jr.'s Dream and You by Carole Boston Weatherford and James E. Ransome. New York: Bloomsbury USA Children's, 2018.

I Have a Dream by Martin Luther King, Jr., and Kadir Nelson. New York: Schwartz & Wade, 2012.

Martin & Mahalia: His Words, Her Song by Andrea David Pinkney and Brian Pinkney. New York: Little, Brown Books for Young Readers, 2013.

Martin's Big Words: The Life of Dr. Martin Luther King, Jr., by Doreen Rappaport and Bryan Collier. New York: Little, Brown Books for Young Readers, 2007.

My Daddy, Dr. Martin Luther King, Jr., by Martin Luther King III and AG Ford. New York: Amistad Press, 2018.

Peaceful Fights for Equal Rights by Rob Sanders and Jared Andrew Schorr. New York: Simon & Schuster Books for Young Readers, 2018.

What Was the March on Washington? by Kathleen Krull and Tim Tomkinson. New York: Penguin Young Readers Group, 2013.

FOR FURTHER READING

"A Day Like No Other: Commemorating the 50th Anniversary of the March on Washington: Preparing for the March." Library of Congress. https://www.loc.gov/exhibits/march-on-washington/preparing-for-the-march.html

100 Amazing Facts About the Negro by Henry Louis Gates, Jr. New York: Pantheon Books, 2017.

Gay and Lesbian History for Kids: The Century-Long Struggle for LGBT Rights by Jerome Pohlen. Chicago: Chicago Review Press, 2016.

The Gay Revolution: The Story of the Struggle by Lillian Faderman. New York: Simon & Schuster Paperbacks, 2015.

I Must Resist: Bayard Rustin's Life in Letters, edited by Michael G. Long. San Francisco: City Lights Books, 2012.

A Queer History of the United States by Michael Bronski. Boston: Beacon Press, 2011.

Troublemaker for Justice: The Story of Bayard Rustin, The Man Behind the March on Washington by Jacqueline Houtman, Walter Naegle, and Michael G. Long. San Francisco: City Lights Books, 2019.

We Are One: The Story of Bayard Rustin by Larry Dane Brimmer. Honesdale, PA: Calkins Creek, 2007.

To all the teachers who taught me to love
books, history, and music. —RS

For the unsung and the undefeated. —CBW

I would like to dedicate this book to Tootie, Tricia, and Willie, who taught
me that every part of my Blackness was beautiful. —BM

Thanks to Walter Naegle for his kind and
helpful assistance with this project.

Henry Holt and Company, *Publishers since 1866*
Henry Holt® is a registered trademark of Macmillan Publishing Group, LLC
120 Broadway, New York, NY 10271 · mackids.com

Our books may be purchased in bulk for promotional, educational, or business use. Please contact your local bookseller or the Macmillan
Corporate and Premium Sales Department at (800) 221-7945 ext. 5442 or by email at MacmillanSpecialMarkets@macmillan.com.

Library of Congress Cataloging-in-Publication Data

Names: Weatherford, Carole Boston, 1956– author. | Sanders, Rob, 1958– author. | McCray, Byron, illustrator.
Title: A song for the unsung : Bayard Rustin, the man behind the 1963 March on Washington /
Carole Boston Weatherford & Rob Sanders ; illustrated by Byron McCray.
Other titles: Bayard Rustin, the man behind the 1963 March on Washington
Description: First edition. | New York : Henry Holt Books for Young Readers, 2022. | Audience: Ages 6–10 | Audience: Grades 2–3 | Summary:
"The author of Moses: When Harriet Tubman Led Her People to Freedom and the author of Pride: The Story of Harvey Milk and the Rainbow
Flag combine their tremendous talents for a singular picture book biography of Bayard Rustin, the gay Black man behind the March on
Washington of 1963"—Provided by publisher.
Identifiers: LCCN 2022017327 | ISBN 9781250779502 (hardcover)
Subjects: LCSH: Rustin, Bayard, 1912-1987—Juvenile literature. | Civil rights workers—United States—Juvenile literature. | African American
civil rights workers—Juvenile literature. | African Americans—Civil rights—History—20th century—Juvenile literature. | Civil rights
movements—United States—Songs and music—Juvenile literature. | Civil rights movements—United States—History—20th century—
Juvenile literature. | United States—Race relations—History—20th century—Juvenile literature.
Classification: LCC E185.97.R93 W43 2022 | DDC 323.092 [B]—dc23/eng/20220506
LC record available at https://lccn.loc.gov/2022017327

First edition, 2022
Book design by Aram Kim and Melisa Vuong
Byron McCray composed the illustrations for this book using a concert of
acrylics, decorative and handmade papers, newspaper, and sheet music on canvas.
Printed in China by RR Donnelley Asia Printing Solutions Ltd., Dongguan City, Guangdong Province

3 5 7 9 10 8 6 4